© Crown copyright 2022

OGL

This publication is licensed under the terms of the Open Government Licence v3.0 except where otherwise stated. To view this licence, visit nationalarchives.gov.uk/doc/open-government-licence/ version/3 or write to the Information Policy Team, The National Archives, Kew, London TW9 4DU, or email: psi@nationalarchives.gsi.gov.uk.Where we haveidentified any third party copyright information you will need to obtain permission from thecopyright holders concerned. This publication is available at www.gov.uk/ government/ publications

ISBN: 9798416596781 (print)

Republished in the UK by Live in The UK Publishing

Human Rights Act 1998

CHAPTER 42

HUMAN RIGHTS ACT 1998

Changes to legislation: *There are currently no known outstanding*
effects for the Human Rights Act 1998. (See end of Document for details)

SCHEDULES

ARTICLE 2

RIGHT TO LIFE

1   Everyone's right to life shall be protected by law. No...
2   Deprivation of life shall not be regarded as inflicted in...

ARTICLE 3

PROHIBITION OF TORTURE

ARTICLE 4

PROHIBITION OF SLAVERY AND FORCED LABOUR

1   No one shall be held in slavery or servitude.
2   No one shall be required to perform forced or compulsory...
3   For the purpose of this Article the term "forced or...

ARTICLE 5

RIGHT TO LIBERTY AND SECURITY

1   Everyone has the right to liberty and security of person....
2   Everyone who is arrested shall be informed promptly, in a...
3   Everyone arrested or detained in accordance with the provisions of...
4   Everyone who is deprived of his liberty by arrest or...
5   Everyone who has been the victim of arrest or detention...

Changes to legislation: *There are currently no known outstanding*
effects for the Human Rights Act 1998. (See end of Document for details)

Human Rights Act 1998 (c. 42)
Document Generated: 2021-08-20

v

Changes to legislation: *There are currently no known outstanding*
effects for the Human Rights Act 1998. (See end of Document for details)

Human Rights Act 1998

1998 CHAPTER 42

An Act to give further effect to rights and freedoms guaranteed under the European
Convention on Human Rights; to make provision with respect to holders of certain
judicial offices who become judges of the European Court of Human Rights; and for
connected purposes.   [9th November 1998]

Be it enacted by the Queen's most Excellent Majesty, by and with the advice and consent of the
Lords Spiritual and Temporal, and Commons, in this present Parliament assembled, and by the
authority of the same, as follows:—

Extent Information

E1   For the extent of this Act outside the U.K., see s. 22(6)(7)

Modifications etc. (not altering text)

C1   Act: certain functions of the Secretary of State transferred to the Lord Chancellor (26.11.2001) by S.I.
2001/3500, arts. 3, 4, **Sch. 1 para. 5**

C2   Act (except ss. 5, 10, 18, 19 and Sch. 4): functions of the Lord Chancellor transferred to the Secretary
of State, and all property, rights and liabilities to which the Lord Chancellor is entitled or subject to
in connection with any such function transferred to the Secretary of State for Constitutional Affairs
(19.8.2003) by S.I. 2003/1887, art. 4, **Sch. 1**

C3   Act modified (30.1.2020) by Direct Payments to Farmers (Legislative Continuity) Act 2020 (c. 2), **ss.
2(8), 9(3)**

C4   Act modified (31.12.2020) by European Union (Withdrawal) Act 2018 (c. 16), s. 25(4), **Sch. 8 para.
30** (with s. 19, Sch. 8 para. 37); S.I. 2020/1622, reg. 3(n)

Introduction

1   The Convention Rights.

(1) In this Act "the Convention rights" means the rights and fundamental freedoms set
out in—

    (a)   Articles 2 to 12 and 14 of the Convention,

    (b)   Articles 1 to 3 of the First Protocol, and

    (c)   [^{F1}Article 1 of the Thirteenth Protocol],

as read with Articles 16 to 18 of the Convention.

(2) Those Articles are to have effect for the purposes of this Act subject to any designated derogation or reservation (as to which see sections 14 and 15).

(3) The Articles are set out in Schedule 1.

(4) The [^{F2}Secretary of State] may by order make such amendments to this Act as he considers appropriate to reflect the effect, in relation to the United Kingdom, of a protocol.

(5) In subsection (4) "protocol" means a protocol to the Convention—

    (a)   which the United Kingdom has ratified; or

    (b)   which the United Kingdom has signed with a view to ratification.

(6) No amendment may be made by an order under subsection (4) so as to come into force before the protocol concerned is in force in relation to the United Kingdom.

Textual Amendments

F1   Words in s. 1(1)(c) substituted (22.6.2004) by The Human Rights Act 1998 (Amendment) Order 2004 (S. I. 2004/1574), **art. 2(1)**

F2   Words in s. 1 substituted (19.8.2003) by The Secretary of State for Constitutional Affairs Order 2003 (S. I. 2003/1887), art. 9, **Sch. 2 para. 10(1)**

2   Interpretation of Convention rights.

(1) A court or tribunal determining a question which has arisen in connection with a Convention right must take into account any—

    (a)   judgment, decision, declaration or advisory opinion of the European Court of Human Rights,

    (b)   opinion of the Commission given in a report adopted under Article 31 of the Convention,

    (c)   decision of the Commission in connection with Article 26 or 27(2) of the Convention, or

    (d)   decision of the Committee of Ministers taken under Article 46 of the Convention,

whenever made or given, so far as, in the opinion of the court or tribunal, it is relevant to the proceedings in which that question has arisen.

(2) Evidence of any judgment, decision, declaration or opinion of which account may have to be taken under this section is to be given in proceedings before any court or tribunal in such manner as may be provided by rules.

(3) In this section "rules" means rules of court or, in the case of proceedings before a tribunal, rules made for the purposes of this section—

    (a)   by ^{F3} . . . [^{F4}the Lord Chancellor or] the Secretary of State, in relation to any proceedings outside Scotland;

    (b)   by the Secretary of State, in relation to proceedings in Scotland; or

(c)   by a Northern Ireland department, in relation to proceedings before a tribunal
in Northern Ireland—
(i) which deals with transferred matters; and
(ii) for which no rules made under paragraph (a) are in force.

Textual Amendments

F3   Words in s. 2(3)(a) repealed (19.8.2003) by The Secretary of State for Constitutional Affairs Order
2003 (S. I. 2003/1887), art. 9, **Sch. 2 para. 10(2)**

F4   Words in s. 2(3)(a) inserted (12.1.2006) by The Transfer of Functions (Lord Chancellor and Secretary
of State) Order 2005 (S.I. 2005/3429), art. 8, **Sch. para. 3**

Modifications etc. (not altering text)

C5   S. 2(3)(a): functions of the Secretary of State to be exercisable concurrently with the Lord Chancellor
(12.1.2006) by The Transfer of Functions (Lord Chancellor and Secretary of State) Order 2005 (S.I.
2005/3429), **art. 3(2)** (with arts. 4, 5)

Legislation

3   Interpretation of legislation.

(1) So far as it is possible to do so, primary legislation and subordinate legislation must
be read and given effect in a way which is compatible with the Convention rights.

(2) This section—
(a)   applies to primary legislation and subordinate legislation whenever enacted;
(b)   does not affect the validity, continuing operation or enforcement of any
incompatible primary legislation; and
(c)   does not affect the validity, continuing operation or enforcement of any
incompatible subordinate legislation if (disregarding any possibility of
revocation) primary legislation prevents removal of the incompatibility.

4   Declaration of incompatibility.

(1) Subsection (2) applies in any proceedings in which a court determines whether a
provision of primary legislation is compatible with a Convention right.

(2) If the court is satisfied that the provision is incompatible with a Convention right, it
may make a declaration of that incompatibility.

(3) Subsection (4) applies in any proceedings in which a court determines whether a
provision of subordinate legislation, made in the exercise of a power conferred by
primary legislation, is compatible with a Convention right.

(4) If the court is satisfied—
(a)   that the provision is incompatible with a Convention right, and
(b)   that (disregarding any possibility of revocation) the primary legislation
concerned prevents removal of the incompatibility,
it may make a declaration of that incompatibility.

(5) In this section "court" means—

$[^{F5}$(a)	the Supreme Court;]
(b)	the Judicial Committee of the Privy Council;
(c)	the $[^{F6}$Court Martial Appeal Court] ;
(d)	in Scotland, the High Court of Justiciary sitting otherwise than as a trial court or the Court of Session;
(e)	in England and Wales or Northern Ireland, the High Court or the Court of Appeal.
$[^{F7}$(f)	the Court of Protection, in any matter being dealt with by the President of the Family Division, the $[^{F8}$Chancellor of the High Court] or a puisne judge of the High Court.]

(6) A declaration under this section ("a declaration of incompatibility")—

    (a)   does not affect the validity, continuing operation or enforcement of the provision in respect of which it is given; and

    (b)   is not binding on the parties to the proceedings in which it is made.

Textual Amendments

F5   S. 4(5)(a) substituted (1.10.2009) by Constitutional Reform Act 2005 (c. 4), ss. 40, 148, **Sch. 9 para. 66(2)**; S.I. 2009/1604, **art. 2(d)**

F6   Words in s. 4(5)(c) substituted (28.3.2009 for certain purposes and 31.10.2009 otherwise) by Armed Forces Act 2006 (c. 52), ss. 378, 383, **Sch. 16 para. 156**; S.I. 2009/812, **art. 3** (with transitional provisions in S.I. 2009/1059); S.I. 2009/1167, **art. 4**

F7   S. 4(5)(f) inserted (1.10.2007) by Mental Capacity Act 2005 (c. 9), ss. 67(1), 68(1)-(3), **Sch. 6 para. 43** (with ss. 27, 28, 29, 62); S.I. 2007/1897, **art. 2(1)(c)(d)**

F8   Words in s. 4(5)(f) substituted (1.10.2013) by Crime and Courts Act 2013 (c. 22), s. 61(3), **Sch. 14 para. 5(5)**; S.I. 2013/2200, **art. 3(g)**

5   **Right of Crown to intervene.**

(1) Where a court is considering whether to make a declaration of incompatibility, the Crown is entitled to notice in accordance with rules of court.

(2) In any case to which subsection (1) applies—

    (a)   a Minister of the Crown (or a person nominated by him),

    (b)   a member of the Scottish Executive,

    (c)   a Northern Ireland Minister,

    (d)   a Northern Ireland department,

is entitled, on giving notice in accordance with rules of court, to be joined as a party to the proceedings.

(3) Notice under subsection (2) may be given at any time during the proceedings.

(4) A person who has been made a party to criminal proceedings (other than in Scotland) as the result of a notice under subsection (2) may, with leave, appeal to the $[^{F9}$Supreme Court] against any declaration of incompatibility made in the proceedings.

(5) In subsection (4)—

         "criminal proceedings" includes all proceedings before the $[^{F10}$Court Martial Appeal Court]; and "leave" means leave granted by the court making the declaration of incompatibility or by the [^{F11}Supreme Court]

Textual Amendments

F9   Words in s. 5(4) substituted (1.10.2009) by Constitutional Reform Act 2005 (c. 4), ss. 40, 148, **Sch. 9 para. 66(3)**; S.I. 2009/1604, **art. 2(d)**

F10   Words in s. 5(5) substituted (28.3.2009 for certain purposes and 31.10.2009 otherwise) by Armed Forces Act 2006 (c. 52), ss. 378, 383, **Sch. 16 para. 157**; S.I. 2009/812, **art. 3** (with transitional provisions in S.I. 2009/1059); S.I. 2009/1167, **art. 4**

F11   Words in s. 5(5) substituted (1.10.2009) by Constitutional Reform Act 2005 (c. 4), ss. 40, 148, **Sch. 9 para. 66(3)**; S.I. 2009/1604, **art. 2(d)**

Modifications etc. (not altering text)

C6   S. 5(2) functions made exercisable concurrently or jointly with the Welsh Ministers by 2006 c. 32, Sch. 3A para. 1 (as inserted (1.4.2018) by Wales Act 2017 (c. 4), s. 71(4), **Sch. 4 para. 1** (with Sch. 7 paras. 1, 6); S.I. 2017/1179, reg. 3(p))

Public authorities

6   **Acts of public authorities.**

(1) It is unlawful for a public authority to act in a way which is incompatible with a Convention right.

(2) Subsection (1) does not apply to an act if—

   (a)   as the result of one or more provisions of primary legislation, the authority could not have acted differently; or

   (b)   in the case of one or more provisions of, or made under, primary legislation which cannot be read or given effect in a way which is compatible with the Convention rights, the authority was acting so as to give effect to or enforce those provisions.

(3) In this section "public authority" includes—

   (a)   a court or tribunal, and

   (b)   any person certain of whose functions are functions of a public nature,

but does not include either House of Parliament or a person exercising functions in connection with proceedings in Parliament.

(4) ^{F12}. . . . .

(5) In relation to a particular act, a person is not a public authority by virtue only of subsection (3)(b) if the nature of the act is private.

(6) "An act" includes a failure to act but does not include a failure to—

   (a)   introduce in, or lay before, Parliament a proposal for legislation; or

   (b)   make any primary legislation or remedial order.

Textual Amendments

F12 S. 6(4) repealed (1.10.2009) by Constitutional Reform Act 2005 (c. 4), ss. 40, 146, 148, Sch. 9 para. 66(4), **Sch. 18 Pt. 5**; S.I. 2009/1604, **art. 2(d)(f)**

Modifications etc. (not altering text)

C7 S. 6 excluded (5.3.2015) by Infrastructure Act 2015 (c. 7), ss. 8(3)(b), 57(1); S.I. 2015/481, reg. 2(a)

C8 S. 6(1) applied (2.10.2000) by 1999 c. 33, ss. 65(2), 170(4); S.I. 2000/2444, art. 2, **Sch. 1** (subject to transitional provisions in arts. 3, 4, Sch. 2)

C9 S. 6(3)(b) modified (1.12.2008 with exception in art. 2(2) of commencing S.I.) by Health and Social Care Act 2008 (c. 14), ss. 145(1)-(4), 170 (with s. 145(5)); S.I. 2008/2994, **art. 2(1)**

C10 S. 6(3)(b) applied (1.4.2015) by Care Act 2014 (c. 23), s. 73(2)(3)127; S.I. 2015/993, art. 2(r) (with transitional provisions in S.I. 2015/995)

7 Proceedings.

(1) A person who claims that a public authority has acted (or proposes to act) in a way which is made unlawful by section 6(1) may—

   (a) bring proceedings against the authority under this Act in the appropriate court or tribunal, or

   (b) rely on the Convention right or rights concerned in any legal proceedings,

but only if he is (or would be) a victim of the unlawful act.

(2) In subsection (1)(a) "appropriate court or tribunal" means such court or tribunal as may be determined in accordance with rules; and proceedings against an authority include a counterclaim or similar proceeding.

(3) If the proceedings are brought on an application for judicial review, the applicant is to be taken to have a sufficient interest in relation to the unlawful act only if he is, or would be, a victim of that act.

(4) If the proceedings are made by way of a petition for judicial review in Scotland, the applicant shall be taken to have title and interest to sue in relation to the unlawful act only if he is, or would be, a victim of that act.

(5) Proceedings under subsection (1)(a) must be brought before the end of—

   (a) the period of one year beginning with the date on which the act complained of took place; or

   (b) such longer period as the court or tribunal considers equitable having regard to all the circumstances,

but that is subject to any rule imposing a stricter time limit in relation to the procedure in question.

(6) In subsection (1)(b) "legal proceedings" includes—

   (a) proceedings brought by or at the instigation of a public authority; and

   (b) an appeal against the decision of a court or tribunal.

(7) For the purposes of this section, a person is a victim of an unlawful act only if he would be a victim for the purposes of Article 34 of the Convention if proceedings were brought in the European Court of Human Rights in respect of that act.

(8) Nothing in this Act creates a criminal offence.

(9) In this section "rules" means—

    (a)   in relation to proceedings before a court or tribunal outside Scotland, rules made by ^{F13}. . . [^{F14}the Lord Chancellor or] the Secretary of State for the purposes of this section or rules of court,

    (b)   in relation to proceedings before a court or tribunal in Scotland, rules made by the Secretary of State for those purposes,

    (c)   in relation to proceedings before a tribunal in Northern Ireland—

        (i) which deals with transferred matters; and

        (ii) for which no rules made under paragraph (a) are in force,

    rules made by a Northern Ireland department for those purposes,

and includes provision made by order under section 1 of the ^{M1}Courts and Legal Services Act 1990.

(10) In making rules, regard must be had to section 9.

(11) The Minister who has power to make rules in relation to a particular tribunal may, to the extent he considers it necessary to ensure that the tribunal can provide an appropriate remedy in relation to an act (or proposed act) of a public authority which is (or would be) unlawful as a result of section 6(1), by order add to—

    (a)   the relief or remedies which the tribunal may grant; or

    (b)   the grounds on which it may grant any of them.

(12) An order made under subsection (11) may contain such incidental, supplemental, consequential or transitional provision as the Minister making it considers appropriate.

(13) "The Minister" includes the Northern Ireland department concerned.

Textual Amendments

F13   Words in s. 7(9)(a) repealed (19.8.2003) by The Secretary of State for Constitutional Affairs Order 2003 (S. I. 2003/1887), art. 9, **Sch. 2 para. 10(2)**

F14   Words in s. 7(9)(a) inserted (12.1.2006) by The Transfer of Functions (Lord Chancellor and Secretary of State) Order 2005 (S.I. 2005/3429), art. 8, **Sch. para. 3,**

Modifications etc. (not altering text)

C11   S. 7 amended (2.10.2000) by Regulation of Investigatory Powers Act 2000 (c. 23), **ss. 65(2)(a), 83** (with s. 82(3); S.I. 2000/2543, **art. 3**

C12   S. 7: referred to (11.3.2005) by Prevention of Terrorism Act 2005 (c. 2), {s. 11(2)}

C13   S. 7(9)(a): functions of the Secretary of State to be exercisable concurrently with the Lord Chancellor (12.1.2006) by The Transfer of Functions (Lord Chancellor and Secretary of State) Order 2005 (S.I. 2005/3429), **art. 3(2)** (with arts. 4, 5)

C14   S. 7(11): functions of the Secretary of State to be exercisable concurrently with the Lord Chancellor (12.1.2006) by The Transfer of Functions (Lord Chancellor and Secretary of State) Order 2005 (S.I. 2005/3429), **art. 3(2)** (with arts. 4, 5)

Marginal Citations

M1   1990 c. 41.

[^{F15}**7A** **Limitation: overseas armed forces proceedings**

(1) A court or tribunal exercising its discretion under section 7(5)(b) in respect of overseas armed forces proceedings must do so—

    (a)   in accordance with subsection (2), and

    (b)   subject to the rule in subsection (4).

(2) The court or tribunal must have particular regard to—

    (a)   the effect of the delay in bringing proceedings on the cogency of evidence adduced or likely to be adduced by the parties, with particular reference to—

        (i) the likely impact of the operational context on the ability of individuals who are (or, at the time of the events to which the proceedings relate, were) members of Her Majesty's forces to remember relevant events or actions fully or accurately, and

        (ii) the extent of dependence on the memories of such individuals, taking into account the effect of the operational context on the ability of such individuals to record, or to retain records of, relevant events or actions;

    (b)   the likely impact of the proceedings on the mental health of any witness or potential witness who is (or, at the time of the events to which the proceedings relate, was) a member of Her Majesty's forces.

(3) In subsection (2) references to "the operational context" are to the fact that the events to which the proceedings relate took place in the context of overseas operations, and include references to the exceptional demands and stresses to which members of Her Majesty's forces are subject.

(4) The rule referred to in subsection (1)(b) is that overseas armed forces proceedings must be brought before the later of—

    (a)   the end of the period of 6 years beginning with the date on which the act complained of took place;

    (b)   the end of the period of 12 months beginning with the date of knowledge.

(5) In subsection (4), the "date of knowledge" means the date on which the person bringing the proceedings first knew, or first ought to have known, both—

    (a)   of the act complained of, and

    (b)   that it was an act of the Ministry of Defence or the Secretary of State for Defence.

(6) "Overseas armed forces proceedings" means proceedings—

    (a)   against the Ministry of Defence or the Secretary of State for Defence, and

    (b)   in connection with overseas operations.

(7) "Overseas operations" means any operations outside the British Islands, including peacekeeping operations and operations for dealing with terrorism, civil unrest or serious public disorder, in the course of which members of Her Majesty's forces come under attack or face the threat of attack or violent resistance.

(8) In this section the reference to the British Islands includes the territorial sea adjacent to the United Kingdom and the territorial sea adjacent to any of the Channel Islands or the Isle of Man.

(9) In this section "Her Majesty's forces" has the same meaning as in the Armed Forces Act 2006 (see section 374 of that Act).]

Changes to legislation: There are currently no known outstanding
effects for the Human Rights Act 1998. (See end of Document for details)

Textual Amendments

F15 S. 7A inserted (30.6.2021) by Overseas Operations (Service Personnel and Veterans) Act 2021 (c. 23),
ss. **11(2)**, 14(2); S.I. 2021/678, reg. 2

8   Judicial remedies.

(1) In relation to any act (or proposed act) of a public authority which the court finds is (or would be) unlawful, it may grant such relief or remedy, or make such order, within its powers as it considers just and appropriate.

(2) But damages may be awarded only by a court which has power to award damages, or to order the payment of compensation, in civil proceedings.

(3) No award of damages is to be made unless, taking account of all the circumstances of the case, including—

  (a)   any other relief or remedy granted, or order made, in relation to the act in question (by that or any other court), and

  (b)   the consequences of any decision (of that or any other court) in respect of that act,

the court is satisfied that the award is necessary to afford just satisfaction to the person in whose favour it is made.

(4) In determining—

  (a)   whether to award damages, or

  (b)   the amount of an award,

the court must take into account the principles applied by the European Court of Human Rights in relation to the award of compensation under Article 41 of the Convention.

(5) A public authority against which damages are awarded is to be treated—

  (a)   in Scotland, for the purposes of section 3 of the [M2]Law Reform (Miscellaneous Provisions) (Scotland) Act 1940 as if the award were made in an action of damages in which the authority has been found liable in respect of loss or damage to the person to whom the award is made;

  (b)   for the purposes of the [M3]Civil Liability (Contribution) Act 1978 as liable in respect of damage suffered by the person to whom the award is made.

(6) In this section—

        "court" includes a tribunal;

        "damages" means damages for an unlawful act of a public authority; and

        "unlawful" means unlawful under section 6(1).

Marginal Citations

M2   1940 c. 42.

M3   1978 c. 47.

9   Judicial acts.

(1) Proceedings under section 7(1)(a) in respect of a judicial act may be brought only—

    (a)   by exercising a right of appeal;

    (b)   on an application (in Scotland a petition) for judicial review; or

    (c)   in such other forum as may be prescribed by rules.

(2) That does not affect any rule of law which prevents a court from being the subject of judicial review.

[F16(3) In proceedings under this Act in respect of a judicial act done in good faith, damages may not be awarded otherwise than—

    (a)   to compensate a person to the extent required by Article 5(5) of the Convention, or

    (b)   to compensate a person for a judicial act that is incompatible with Article 6 of the Convention in circumstances where the person is detained and, but for the incompatibility, the person would not have been detained or would not have been detained for so long.]

(4) An award of damages permitted by subsection (3) is to be made against the Crown; but no award may be made unless the appropriate person, if not a party to the proceedings, is joined.

(5) In this section—

    "appropriate person" means the Minister responsible for the court concerned, or a person or government department nominated by him;

    "court" includes a tribunal;

    "judge" includes a member of a tribunal, a justice of the peace [F17(or, in Northern Ireland, a lay magistrate)] and a clerk or other officer entitled to exercise the jurisdiction of a court;

    "judicial act" means a judicial act of a court and includes an act done on the instructions, or on behalf, of a judge; and

    "rules" has the same meaning as in section 7(9).

Textual Amendments

F16 S. 9(3) substituted (21.10.2020) by The Human Rights Act 1998 (Remedial) Order 2020 (S.I. 2020/1160), arts. 1(2), **2(1)** (with art. 2(2))

F17 Words in definition s. 9(5) inserted (N.I.)(1.4.2005) by 2002 c. 26, s. 10(6), Sch. 4 para. 39; S.R. 2005/109, **art. 2 Sch.**

Remedial action

10   Power to take remedial action.

(1) This section applies if—

    (a)   a provision of legislation has been declared under section 4 to be incompatible with a Convention right and, if an appeal lies—

        (i) all persons who may appeal have stated in writing that they do not intend to do so;

Human Rights Act 1998 (c. 42)
Document Generated: 2021-08-18

11

Changes to legislation: *There are currently no known outstanding*
effects for the Human Rights Act 1998. (See end of Document for details)

    (ii) the time for bringing an appeal has expired and no appeal has been brought within that time; or

    (iii) an appeal brought within that time has been determined or abandoned; or

(b) it appears to a Minister of the Crown or Her Majesty in Council that, having regard to a finding of the European Court of Human Rights made after the coming into force of this section in proceedings against the United Kingdom, a provision of legislation is incompatible with an obligation of the United Kingdom arising from the Convention.

(2) If a Minister of the Crown considers that there are compelling reasons for proceeding under this section, he may by order make such amendments to the legislation as he considers necessary to remove the incompatibility.

(3) If, in the case of subordinate legislation, a Minister of the Crown considers—

(a) that it is necessary to amend the primary legislation under which the subordinate legislation in question was made, in order to enable the incompatibility to be removed, and

(b) that there are compelling reasons for proceeding under this section,

he may by order make such amendments to the primary legislation as he considers necessary.

(4) This section also applies where the provision in question is in subordinate legislation and has been quashed, or declared invalid, by reason of incompatibility with a Convention right and the Minister proposes to proceed under paragraph 2(b) of Schedule 2.

(5) If the legislation is an Order in Council, the power conferred by subsection (2) or (3) is exercisable by Her Majesty in Council.

(6) In this section "legislation" does not include a Measure of the Church Assembly or of the General Synod of the Church of England.

(7) Schedule 2 makes further provision about remedial orders.

Other rights and proceedings

11   Safeguard for existing human rights.

A person's reliance on a Convention right does not restrict—

(a) any other right or freedom conferred on him by or under any law having effect in any part of the United Kingdom; or

(b) his right to make any claim or bring any proceedings which he could make or bring apart from sections 7 to 9.

12   Freedom of expression.

(1) This section applies if a court is considering whether to grant any relief which, if granted, might affect the exercise of the Convention right to freedom of expression.

(2) If the person against whom the application for relief is made ("the respondent") is neither present nor represented, no such relief is to be granted unless the court is satisfied—

12

Human Rights Act 1998 (c. 42)
Document Generated: 2021-08-18

*Changes to legislation: There are currently no known outstanding
effects for the Human Rights Act 1998. (See end of Document for details)*

(a) that the applicant has taken all practicable steps to notify the respondent; or

(b) that there are compelling reasons why the respondent should not be notified.

(3) No such relief is to be granted so as to restrain publication before trial unless the court is satisfied that the applicant is likely to establish that publication should not be allowed.

(4) The court must have particular regard to the importance of the Convention right to freedom of expression and, where the proceedings relate to material which the respondent claims, or which appears to the court, to be journalistic, literary or artistic material (or to conduct connected with such material), to—

(a) the extent to which—

(i) the material has, or is about to, become available to the public; or

(ii) it is, or would be, in the public interest for the material to be published;

(b) any relevant privacy code.

(5) In this section—

"court" includes a tribunal; and

"relief" includes any remedy or order (other than in criminal proceedings).

13 Freedom of thought, conscience and religion.

(1) If a court's determination of any question arising under this Act might affect the exercise by a religious organisation (itself or its members collectively) of the Convention right to freedom of thought, conscience and religion, it must have particular regard to the importance of that right.

(2) In this section "court" includes a tribunal.

Derogations and reservations

14 Derogations.

(1) In this Act "designated derogation" means—

F18
. . . .

any derogation by the United Kingdom from an Article of the Convention, or of any protocol to the Convention, which is designated for the purposes of this Act in an order made by the [F19Secretary of State]

F20(2) . . . .

(3) If a designated derogation is amended or replaced it ceases to be a designated derogation.

(4) But subsection (3) does not prevent the [F21Secretary of State] from exercising his power under subsection (1) F22. . . to make a fresh designation order in respect of the Article concerned.

(5) The [F23Secretary of State] must by order make such amendments to Schedule 3 as he considers appropriate to reflect—

(a) any designation order; or

(b) the effect of subsection (3).

(6) A designation order may be made in anticipation of the making by the United Kingdom of a proposed derogation.

Textual Amendments

F18 S. 14(1): from "(a)" to "(b)" repealed (1.4.2001) by S.I. 2001/1216, **art. 2(a)**

F19 Words in s. 14 substituted (19.8.2003) by The Secretary of State for Constitutional Affairs Order 2003 (S. I. 2003/1887), art. 9, **Sch. 2 para. 10(1)**

F20 S. 14(2) repealed (1.4.2001) by S.I. 2001/1216, **art. 2(b)**

F21 Words in s. 14 substituted (19.8.2003) by The Secretary of State for Constitutional Affairs Order 2003 (S. I. 2003/1887), art. 9, **Sch. 2 para. 10(1)**

F22 S. 14(4): "(b)" repealed (1.4.2001) by S.I. 2001/1216, **art. 2(c)**

F23 Words in s. 14 substituted (19.8.2003) by The Secretary of State for Constitutional Affairs Order 2003 (S. I. 2003/1887), art. 9, **Sch. 2 para. 10(1)**

15   Reservations.

(1) In this Act "designated reservation" means—

    (a)   the United Kingdom's reservation to Article 2 of the First Protocol to the Convention; and

    (b)   any other reservation by the United Kingdom to an Article of the Convention, or of any protocol to the Convention, which is designated for the purposes of this Act in an order made by the [F24Secretary of State] .

(2) The text of the reservation referred to in subsection (1)(a) is set out in Part II of Schedule 3.

(3) If a designated reservation is withdrawn wholly or in part it ceases to be a designated reservation.

(4) But subsection (3) does not prevent the [F25Secretary of State] from exercising his power under subsection (1)(b) to make a fresh designation order in respect of the Article concerned.

(5) [F26Secretary of State] must by order make such amendments to this Act as he considers appropriate to reflect—

    (a)   any designation order; or

    (b)   the effect of subsection (3).

Textual Amendments

F24 Words in s. 15 substituted (19.8.2003) by The Secretary of State for Constitutional Affairs Order 2003 (S. I. 2003/1887), art. 9, **Sch. 2 para. 10(1)**

F25 Words in s. 15 substituted (19.8.2003) by The Secretary of State for Constitutional Affairs Order 2003 (S. I. 2003/1887), art. 9, **Sch. 2 para. 10(1)**

F26 Words in s. 15 substituted (19.8.2003) by The Secretary of State for Constitutional Affairs Order 2003 (S. I. 2003/1887), art. 9, **Sch. 2 para. 10(1)**

16   Period for which designated derogations have effect.

(1) If it has not already been withdrawn by the United Kingdom, a designated derogation ceases to have effect for the purposes of this Act—

F27
. . . .

. . ., at the end of the period of five years beginning with the date on which the order designating it was made.

(2) At any time before the period—

(a)   fixed by subsection (1) ^{F28}. . ., or

(b)   extended by an order under this subsection,

comes to an end, the [^{F29}Secretary of State] may by order extend it by a further period of five years.

(3) An order under section 14(1) ^{F30}. . . ceases to have effect at the end of the period for consideration, unless a resolution has been passed by each House approving the order.

(4) Subsection (3) does not affect—

(a)   anything done in reliance on the order; or

(b)   the power to make a fresh order under section 14(1) ^{F30}. . ..

(5) In subsection (3) "period for consideration" means the period of forty days beginning with the day on which the order was made.

(6) In calculating the period for consideration, no account is to be taken of any time during which—

(a)   Parliament is dissolved or prorogued; or

(b)   both Houses are adjourned for more than four days.

(7) If a designated derogation is withdrawn by the United Kingdom, the [^{F31}Secretary of State] must by order make such amendments to this Act as he considers are required to reflect that withdrawal.

Textual Amendments

F27   S. 16(1): words from "(a)" to "any other derogation" repealed (1.4.2001) by S.I. 2001/1216, **art. 3(a)**

F28   Words in s. 16(2)(a) repealed (1.4.2001) by S.I. 2001/1216, **art. 3(b)**

F29   Words in s. 16 substituted (19.8.2003) by The Secretary of State for Constitutional Affairs Order 2003 (S. I. 2003/1887), art. 9, **Sch. 2 para. 10(1)**

F30   S. 16(3)(4)(b): "(b)" repealed (1.4.2001) by S.I. 2001/1216, **art. 3(c)(d)**

F31   Words in s. 16 substituted (19.8.2003) by The Secretary of State for Constitutional Affairs Order 2003 (S. I. 2003/1887), art. 9, **Sch. 2 para. 10(1)**

17   Periodic review of designated reservations.

(1) The appropriate Minister must review the designated reservation referred to in section 15(1)(a)—

(a)   before the end of the period of five years beginning with the date on which section 1(2) came into force; and

(b)   if that designation is still in force, before the end of the period of five years beginning with the date on which the last report relating to it was laid under subsection (3).

(2) The appropriate Minister must review each of the other designated reservations (if any)—

    (a)   before the end of the period of five years beginning with the date on which the order designating the reservation first came into force; and

    (b)   if the designation is still in force, before the end of the period of five years beginning with the date on which the last report relating to it was laid under subsection (3).

(3) The Minister conducting a review under this section must prepare a report on the result of the review and lay a copy of it before each House of Parliament.

Judges of the European Court of Human Rights

18   Appointment to European Court of Human Rights.

(1) In this section "judicial office" means the office of—

    (a)   Lord Justice of Appeal, Justice of the High Court or Circuit judge, in England and Wales;

    (b)   judge of the Court of Session or sheriff, in Scotland;

    (c)   Lord Justice of Appeal, judge of the High Court or county court judge, in Northern Ireland.

(2) The holder of a judicial office may become a judge of the European Court of Human Rights ("the Court") without being required to relinquish his office.

(3) But he is not required to perform the duties of his judicial office while he is a judge of the Court.

(4) In respect of any period during which he is a judge of the Court—

    (a)   a Lord Justice of Appeal or Justice of the High Court is not to count as a judge of the relevant court for the purposes of section 2(1) or 4(1) of the [F32Senior Courts Act 1981](maximum number of judges) nor as a judge of the [F33Senior Courts] for the purposes of section 12(1) to (6) of that Act (salaries etc.);

    (b)   a judge of the Court of Session is not to count as a judge of that court for the purposes of section 1(1) of the M4Court of Session Act 1988 (maximum number of judges) or of section 9(1)(c) of the M5Administration of Justice Act 1973 ("the 1973 Act") (salaries etc.);

    (c)   a Lord Justice of Appeal or judge of the High Court in Northern Ireland is not to count as a judge of the relevant court for the purposes of section 2(1) or 3(1) of the M6Judicature (Northern Ireland) Act 1978 (maximum number of judges) nor as a judge of the [F34Court of Judicature] of Northern Ireland for the purposes of section 9(1)(d) of the 1973 Act (salaries etc.);

    (d)   a Circuit judge is not to count as such for the purposes of section 18 of the M7Courts Act 1971 (salaries etc.);

    (e)   a sheriff is not to count as such for the purposes of section 14 of the M8Sheriff Courts (Scotland) Act 1907 (salaries etc.);

    (f)   a county court judge of Northern Ireland is not to count as such for the purposes of section 106 of the M9County Courts Act Northern Ireland) 1959 (salaries etc.).

(5) If a sheriff principal is appointed a judge of the Court, section 11(1) of the ^{M10}Sheriff Courts (Scotland) Act 1971 (temporary appointment of sheriff principal) applies, while he holds that appointment, as if his office is vacant.

(6) Schedule 4 makes provision about judicial pensions in relation to the holder of a judicial office who serves as a judge of the Court.

(7) The Lord Chancellor or the Secretary of State may by order make such transitional provision (including, in particular, provision for a temporary increase in the maximum number of judges) as he considers appropriate in relation to any holder of a judicial office who has completed his service as a judge of the Court.

[^{F35}(7A) The following paragraphs apply to the making of an order under subsection (7) in relation to any holder of a judicial office listed in subsection (1)(a)—

    (a) before deciding what transitional provision it is appropriate to make, the person making the order must consult the Lord Chief Justice of England and Wales;

    (b) before making the order, that person must consult the Lord Chief Justice of England and Wales.

(7B) The following paragraphs apply to the making of an order under subsection (7) in relation to any holder of a judicial office listed in subsection (1)(c)—

    (a) before deciding what transitional provision it is appropriate to make, the person making the order must consult the Lord Chief Justice of Northern Ireland;

    (b) before making the order, that person must consult the Lord Chief Justice of Northern Ireland.

(7C) The Lord Chief Justice of England and Wales may nominate a judicial office holder (within the meaning of section 109(4) of the Constitutional Reform Act 2005) to exercise his functions under this section.

(7D) The Lord Chief Justice of Northern Ireland may nominate any of the following to exercise his functions under this section—

    (a) the holder of one of the offices listed in Schedule 1 to the Justice (Northern Ireland) Act 2002;

    (b) a Lord Justice of Appeal (as defined in section 88 of that Act).]

Textual Amendments

F32 Words in s. 18(4)(a) substituted (1.10.2009) by Constitutional Reform Act 2005 (c. 4), ss. 59, 148, Sch. 11 para. 4; S.I. 2009/1604, **art. 2(d)**

F33 Words in s. 18(4)(a) substituted (1.10.2009) by Constitutional Reform Act 2005 (c. 4), ss. 59, 148, Sch. 11 para. 4; S.I. 2009/1604, **art. 2(d)**

F34 Words in s. 18(4)(c) substituted (1.10.2009) by Constitutional Reform Act 2005 (c. 4), ss. 59, 148, Sch. 11 para. 6; S.I. 2009/1604, **art. 2(d)**

F35 S. 18(7A)-(7D) inserted (3.4.2006) by Constitutional Reform Act 2005 (c. 4), ss. 15, 148, **Sch. 4 para. 278**; S.I. 2006/1014, **art. 2, Sch. 1 para. 11(v)**

Marginal Citations

M4 1988 c. 36.

M5 1973 c. 15.

M6 1978 c. 23.

Human Rights Act 1998 (c. 42)
Document Generated: 2021-08-18

17

*Changes to legislation: There are currently no known outstanding
effects for the Human Rights Act 1998. (See end of Document for details)*

M7	1971 c. 23.
M8	1907 c. 51.
M9	1959 c. 25 (N.I.).
M10	1971 c. 58.

Parliamentary procedure

19 Statements of compatibility.

(1) A Minister of the Crown in charge of a Bill in either House of Parliament must, before Second Reading of the Bill—

    (a) make a statement to the effect that in his view the provisions of the Bill are compatible with the Convention rights ("a statement of compatibility"); or

    (b) make a statement to the effect that although he is unable to make a statement of compatibility the government nevertheless wishes the House to proceed with the Bill.

(2) The statement must be in writing and be published in such manner as the Minister making it considers appropriate.

Supplemental

20 Orders etc. under this Act.

(1) Any power of a Minister of the Crown to make an order under this Act is exercisable by statutory instrument.

(2) The power of [F36]. . . [F37the Lord Chancellor or] the Secretary of State to make rules (other than rules of court) under section 2(3) or 7(9) is exercisable by statutory instrument.

(3) Any statutory instrument made under section 14, 15 or 16(7) must be laid before Parliament.

(4) No order may be made by [F38]. . . [F39the Lord Chancellor or] the Secretary of State under section 1(4), 7(11) or 16(2) unless a draft of the order has been laid before, and approved by, each House of Parliament.

(5) Any statutory instrument made under section 18(7) or Schedule 4, or to which subsection (2) applies, shall be subject to annulment in pursuance of a resolution of either House of Parliament.

(6) The power of a Northern Ireland department to make—

    (a) rules under section 2(3)(c) or 7(9)(c), or

    (b) an order under section 7(11),

is exercisable by statutory rule for the purposes of the [M11]Statutory Rules (Northern Ireland) Order 1979.

(7) Any rules made under section 2(3)(c) or 7(9)(c) shall be subject to negative resolution; and section 41(6) of the [M12]Interpretation Act Northern Ireland) 1954 (meaning of "subject to negative resolution") shall apply as if the power to make the rules were conferred by an Act of the Northern Ireland Assembly.

(8) No order may be made by a Northern Ireland department under section 7(11) unless a draft of the order has been laid before, and approved by, the Northern Ireland Assembly.

Textual Amendments

F36 Words in s. 20(2) repealed (19.8.2003) by The Secretary of State for Constitutional Affairs Order 2003 (S. I. 2003/1887), art. 9, **Sch. 2 para. 10(2)**

F37 Words in s. 20(2) inserted (12.1.2006) by The Transfer of Functions (Lord Chancellor and Secretary of State) Order 2005 (S.I. 2005/3429), art. 8, **Sch. para. 3**

F38 Words in s. 20(4) repealed (19.8.2003) by The Secretary of State for Constitutional Affairs Order 2003 (S. I. 2003/1887), art. 9, **Sch. 2 para. 10(2)**

F39 Words in s. 20(4) inserted (12.1.2006) by The Transfer of Functions (Lord Chancellor and Secretary of State) Order 2005 (S.I. 2005/3429), art. 8, **Sch. para. 3**

Marginal Citations

M11 S.I. 1979/1573 (N.I. 12).
M12 1954 c. 33 (N.I.).

21   Interpretation, etc.

(1) In this Act—

"amend" includes repeal and apply (with or without modifications);

"the appropriate Minister" means the Minister of the Crown having charge of the appropriate authorised government department (within the meaning of the [M13]Crown Proceedings Act 1947);

"the Commission" means the European Commission of Human Rights;

"the Convention" means the Convention for the Protection of Human Rights and Fundamental Freedoms, agreed by the Council of Europe at Rome on 4th November 1950 as it has effect for the time being in relation to the United Kingdom;

"declaration of incompatibility" means a declaration under section 4;

"Minister of the Crown" has the same meaning as in the Ministers of the [M14]Crown Act 1975;

"Northern Ireland Minister" includes the First Minister and the deputy First Minister in Northern Ireland;

"primary legislation" means any—

(a) public general Act;

(b) local and personal Act;

(c) private Act;

(d) Measure of the Church Assembly;

(e) Measure of the General Synod of the Church of England;

(f) Order in Council—

(i) made in exercise of Her Majesty's Royal Prerogative;

(ii) made under section 38(1)(a) of the [M15]Northern Ireland Constitution Act 1973 or the corresponding provision of the Northern Ireland Act 1998; or

(iii) amending an Act of a kind mentioned in paragraph (a), (b) or (c);

and includes an order or other instrument made under primary legislation (otherwise than by the [F40Welsh Ministers, the First Minister for Wales, the Counsel General to the Welsh Assembly Government,] a member of the Scottish Executive, a Northern Ireland Minister or a Northern Ireland department) to the extent to which it operates to bring one or more provisions of that legislation into force or amends any primary legislation;

"the First Protocol" means the protocol to the Convention agreed at Paris on 20th March 1952;

F41 . . .

"the Eleventh Protocol" means the protocol to the Convention (restructuring the control machinery established by the Convention) agreed at Strasbourg on 11th May 1994;

[F42"the Thirteenth Protocol" means the protocol to the Convention (concerning the abolition of the death penalty in all circumstances) agreed at Vilnius on 3rd May 2002;]

"remedial order" means an order under section 10;

"subordinate legislation" means any—

(a) Order in Council other than one—

(i) made in exercise of Her Majesty's Royal Prerogative;

(ii) made under section 38(1)(a) of the Northern Ireland Constitution Act 1973 or the corresponding provision of the Northern Ireland Act 1998; or

(iii) amending an Act of a kind mentioned in the definition of primary legislation;

(b) Act of the Scottish Parliament;

(ba) [F43Measure of the National Assembly for Wales;

(bb) Act of the National Assembly for Wales;]

(c) Act of the Parliament of Northern Ireland;

(d) Measure of the Assembly established under section 1 of the M16Northern Ireland Assembly Act 1973;

(e) Act of the Northern Ireland Assembly;

(f) order, rules, regulations, scheme, warrant, byelaw or other instrument made under primary legislation (except to the extent to which it operates to bring one or more provisions of that legislation into force or amends any primary legislation);

(g) order, rules, regulations, scheme, warrant, byelaw or other instrument made under legislation mentioned in paragraph (b), (c), (d) or (e) or made under an Order in Council applying only to Northern Ireland;

(h) order, rules, regulations, scheme, warrant, byelaw or other instrument made by a member of the Scottish Executive [F44, Welsh Ministers, the First Minister for Wales, the Counsel General to the Welsh Assembly Government,] a Northern Ireland Minister or a Northern Ireland department in exercise of prerogative or other executive functions of Her Majesty which are exercisable by such a person on behalf of Her Majesty;

"transferred matters" has the same meaning as in the Northern Ireland Act 1998; and

"tribunal" means any tribunal in which legal proceedings may be brought.

(2) The references in paragraphs (b) and (c) of section 2(1) to Articles are to Articles of the Convention as they had effect immediately before the coming into force of the Eleventh Protocol.

(3) The reference in paragraph (d) of section 2(1) to Article 46 includes a reference to Articles 32 and 54 of the Convention as they had effect immediately before the coming into force of the Eleventh Protocol.

(4) The references in section 2(1) to a report or decision of the Commission or a decision of the Committee of Ministers include references to a report or decision made as provided by paragraphs 3, 4 and 6 of Article 5 of the Eleventh Protocol (transitional provisions).

^{F45}(5) . . . .

Extent Information

E2   For the extent of s. 21 outside the U.K. see s. 22(7)

Textual Amendments

F40   Words in the definition of "primary legislation" in s. 21(1) substituted by Government of Wales Act 2006 (c. 32), s. 160(1), **Sch. 10 para.56(2)** (with Sch. 11 para. 22) the amending provision coming into force immediately after "the 2007 election" (held on 3.5.2007) subject to s. 161(4)(5) of the amending Act, which provides for certain provisions to come into force for specified purposes immediately after the end of "the initial period" (which ended with the day of the first appointment of a First Minister on 25.5.2007) - see ss. 46, 161(1)(4)(5) of the amending Act.

F41   S. 21(1): definition of "the Sixth Protocol" omitted (22.6.2004) by virtue of The Human Rights Act 1998 (Amendment) Order 2004 (S.I. 2004/1574), **art. 2(2)**

F42   S. 21(1): definition of "the Thirteenth Protocol" inserted (22.6.2004) by virtue of The Human Rights Act 1998 (Amendment) Order 2004 (S.I. 2004/1574), **art. 2(2)**

F43   Words in the definition of "subordinate legislation" in s. 21(1) substituted by Government of Wales Act 2006 (c. 32), s. 160(1), **Sch. 10 para.56(3)** (with Sch. 11 para. 22) the amending provision coming into force immediately after "the 2007 election" (held on 3.5.2007) subject to s. 161(4)(5) of the amending Act, which provides for certain provisions to come into force for specified purposes immediately after the end of "the initial period" (which ended with the day of the first appointment of a First Minister on 25.5.2007) - see ss. 46, 161(1)(4)(5) of the amending Act.

F44   Words in the definition of "subordinate legislation" in s. 21(1) substituted by Government of Wales Act 2006 (c. 32), s. 160(1), **Sch. 10 para.56(4)** (with Sch. 11 para. 22) the amending provision coming into force immediately after "the 2007 election" (held on 3.5.2007) subject to s. 161(4)(5) of the amending Act, which provides for certain provisions to come into force for specified purposes immediately after the end of "the initial period" (which ended with the day of the first appointment of a First Minister on 25.5.2007) - see ss. 46, 161(1)(4)(5) of the amending Act.

F45   S. 21(5) repealed (28.3.2009 for specified purposes and 31.10.2009 otherwise) by Armed Forces Act 2006 (c. 52), ss. 378, 383, **Sch. 17**; S.I. 2009/812, **art. 3** (with transitional provisions in S.I. 2009/1059); S.I. 2009/1167, **art. 4**

Commencement Information

I1   S. 21 wholly in force at 2.10.2000; s. 21(5) in force at Royal Assent, see s. 22(2)(3); s. 21 in force so far as not already in force (2.10.2000) by S.I. 2000/1851, **art. 2**

Marginal Citations

M13   1947 c. 44.

M14   1975 c. 26.

M15   1973 c. 36.

M16 1973 c. 17.

22 Short title, commencement, application and extent.

(1) This Act may be cited as the Human Rights Act 1998.

(2) Sections 18, 20 and 21(5) and this section come into force on the passing of this Act.

(3) The other provisions of this Act come into force on such day as the Secretary of State may by order appoint; and different days may be appointed for different purposes.

(4) Paragraph (b) of subsection (1) of section 7 applies to proceedings brought by or at the instigation of a public authority whenever the act in question took place; but otherwise that subsection does not apply to an act taking place before the coming into force of that section.

[F46(4A) Section 7A (limitation: overseas armed forces proceedings) applies to proceedings brought under section 7(1)(a) on or after the date on which section 7A comes into force, whenever the act in question took place.]

(5) This Act binds the Crown.

(6) This Act extends to Northern Ireland.

F47(7) . . . .

Subordinate Legislation Made

P1 S. 22(3) power partly exercised: 24.11.1998 appointed for specified provisions by S.I. 1998/2882, **art. 2**

S. 22(3) power fully exercised: 2.10.2000 appointed for remaining provisions by S.I. 2000/1851, **art. 2**

Textual Amendments

F46 S. 22(4A) inserted (30.6.2021) by Overseas Operations (Service Personnel and Veterans) Act 2021 (c. 23), **ss. 11(3)**, 14(2); S.I. 2021/678, reg. 2

F47 S. 22(7) repealed (28.3.2009 for certain purposes and 31.10.2009 otherwise) by Armed Forces Act 2006 (c. 52), ss. 378, 383, **Sch. 17**; S.I. 2009/812, **art. 3** (with transitional provisions in S.I. 2009/1059); S.I. 2009/1167, **art. 4**

Changes to legislation: *There are currently no known outstanding effects for the Human Rights Act 1998. (See end of Document for details)*

SCHEDULES

SCHEDULE 1   Section 1(3).

THE ARTICLES

PART I

THE CONVENTION

RIGHTS AND FREEDOMS

ARTICLE 2

RIGHT TO LIFE

1   Everyone's right to life shall be protected by law. No one shall be deprived of his life intentionally save in the execution of a sentence of a court following his conviction of a crime for which this penalty is provided by law.

2   Deprivation of life shall not be regarded as inflicted in contravention of this Article when it results from the use of force which is no more than absolutely necessary:

    (a)   in defence of any person from unlawful violence;

    (b)   in order to effect a lawful arrest or to prevent the escape of a person lawfully detained;

    (c)   in action lawfully taken for the purpose of quelling a riot or insurrection.

ARTICLE 3

PROHIBITION OF TORTURE

No one shall be subjected to torture or to inhuman or degrading treatment or punishment.

ARTICLE 4

PROHIBITION OF SLAVERY AND FORCED LABOUR

1   No one shall be held in slavery or servitude.

2   No one shall be required to perform forced or compulsory labour.

3   For the purpose of this Article the term "forced or compulsory labour" shall not include:

    (a)   any work required to be done in the ordinary course of detention imposed according to the provisions of Article 5 of this Convention or during conditional release from such detention;

Changes to legislation: *There are currently no known outstanding effects for the Human Rights Act 1998. (See end of Document for details)*

(b)   any service of a military character or, in case of conscientious objectors in countries where they are recognised, service exacted instead of compulsory military service;

(c)   any service exacted in case of an emergency or calamity threatening the life or well-being of the community;

(d)   any work or service which forms part of normal civic obligations.

ARTICLE 5

RIGHT TO LIBERTY AND SECURITY

1   Everyone has the right to liberty and security of person. No one shall be deprived of his liberty save in the following cases and in accordance with a procedure prescribed by law:

(a)   the lawful detention of a person after conviction by a competent court;

(b)   the lawful arrest or detention of a person for non-compliance with the lawful order of a court or in order to secure the fulfilment of any obligation prescribed by law;

(c)   the lawful arrest or detention of a person effected for the purpose of bringing him before the competent legal authority on reasonable suspicion of having committed an offence or when it is reasonably considered necessary to prevent his committing an offence or fleeing after having done so;

(d)   the detention of a minor by lawful order for the purpose of educational supervision or his lawful detention for the purpose of bringing him before the competent legal authority;

(e)   the lawful detention of persons for the prevention of the spreading of infectious diseases, of persons of unsound mind, alcoholics or drug addicts or vagrants;

(f)   the lawful arrest or detention of a person to prevent his effecting an unauthorised entry into the country or of a person against whom action is being taken with a view to deportation or extradition.

2   Everyone who is arrested shall be informed promptly, in a language which he understands, of the reasons for his arrest and of any charge against him.

3   Everyone arrested or detained in accordance with the provisions of paragraph 1(c) of this Article shall be brought promptly before a judge or other officer authorised by law to exercise judicial power and shall be entitled to trial within a reasonable time or to release pending trial. Release may be conditioned by guarantees to appear for trial.

4   Everyone who is deprived of his liberty by arrest or detention shall be entitled to take proceedings by which the lawfulness of his detention shall be decided speedily by a court and his release ordered if the detention is not lawful.

5   Everyone who has been the victim of arrest or detention in contravention of the provisions of this Article shall have an enforceable right to compensation.

Changes to legislation: There are currently no known outstanding
effects for the Human Rights Act 1998. (See end of Document for details)

ARTICLE 6

RIGHT TO A FAIR TRIAL

1 In the determination of his civil rights and obligations or of any criminal charge against him, everyone is entitled to a fair and public hearing within a reasonable time by an independent and impartial tribunal established by law. Judgment shall be pronounced publicly but the press and public may be excluded from all or part of the trial in the interest of morals, public order or national security in a democratic society, where the interests of juveniles or the protection of the private life of the parties so require, or to the extent strictly necessary in the opinion of the court in special circumstances where publicity would prejudice the interests of justice.

2 Everyone charged with a criminal offence shall be presumed innocent until proved guilty according to law.

3 Everyone charged with a criminal offence has the following minimum rights:
   (a) to be informed promptly, in a language which he understands and in detail, of the nature and cause of the accusation against him;
   (b) to have adequate time and facilities for the preparation of his defence;
   (c) to defend himself in person or through legal assistance of his own choosing or, if he has not sufficient means to pay for legal assistance, to be given it free when the interests of justice so require;
   (d) to examine or have examined witnesses against him and to obtain the attendance and examination of witnesses on his behalf under the same conditions as witnesses against him;
   (e) to have the free assistance of an interpreter if he cannot understand or speak the language used in court.

ARTICLE 7

NO PUNISHMENT WITHOUT LAW

1 No one shall be held guilty of any criminal offence on account of any act or omission which did not constitute a criminal offence under national or international law at the time when it was committed. Nor shall a heavier penalty be imposed than the one that was applicable at the time the criminal offence was committed.

2 This Article shall not prejudice the trial and punishment of any person for any act or omission which, at the time when it was committed, was criminal according to the general principles of law recognised by civilised nations.

ARTICLE 8

RIGHT TO RESPECT FOR PRIVATE AND FAMILY LIFE

1 Everyone has the right to respect for his private and family life, his home and his correspondence.

2 There shall be no interference by a public authority with the exercise of this right except such as is in accordance with the law and is necessary in a democratic society in the interests of national security, public safety or the economic well-being of

Changes to legislation: *There are currently no known outstanding
effects for the Human Rights Act 1998. (See end of Document for details)*

the country, for the prevention of disorder or crime, for the protection of health or morals, or for the protection of the rights and freedoms of others.

ARTICLE 9

FREEDOM OF THOUGHT, CONSCIENCE AND RELIGION

1   Everyone has the right to freedom of thought, conscience and religion; this right includes freedom to change his religion or belief and freedom, either alone or in community with others and in public or private, to manifest his religion or belief, in worship, teaching, practice and observance.

2   Freedom to manifest one's religion or beliefs shall be subject only to such limitations as are prescribed by law and are necessary in a democratic society in the interests of public safety, for the protection of public order, health or morals, or for the protection of the rights and freedoms of others.

ARTICLE 10

FREEDOM OF EXPRESSION

1   Everyone has the right to freedom of expression. This right shall include freedom to hold opinions and to receive and impart information and ideas without interference by public authority and regardless of frontiers. This Article shall not prevent States from requiring the licensing of broadcasting, television or cinema enterprises.

2   The exercise of these freedoms, since it carries with it duties and responsibilities, may be subject to such formalities, conditions, restrictions or penalties as are prescribed by law and are necessary in a democratic society, in the interests of national security, territorial integrity or public safety, for the prevention of disorder or crime, for the protection of health or morals, for the protection of the reputation or rights of others, for preventing the disclosure of information received in confidence, or for maintaining the authority and impartiality of the judiciary.

ARTICLE 11

FREEDOM OF ASSEMBLY AND ASSOCIATION

1   Everyone has the right to freedom of peaceful assembly and to freedom of association with others, including the right to form and to join trade unions for the protection of his interests.

2   No restrictions shall be placed on the exercise of these rights other than such as are prescribed by law and are necessary in a democratic society in the interests of national security or public safety, for the prevention of disorder or crime, for the protection of health or morals or for the protection of the rights and freedoms of others. This Article shall not prevent the imposition of lawful restrictions on the exercise of these rights by members of the armed forces, of the police or of the administration of the State.

ARTICLE 12

RIGHT TO MARRY

Men and women of marriageable age have the right to marry and to found a family, according to the national laws governing the exercise of this right.

ARTICLE 14

PROHIBITION OF DISCRIMINATION

The enjoyment of the rights and freedoms set forth in this Convention shall be secured without discrimination on any ground such as sex, race, colour, language, religion, political or other opinion, national or social origin, association with a national minority, property, birth or other status.

ARTICLE 16

RESTRICTIONS ON POLITICAL ACTIVITY OF ALIENS

Nothing in Articles 10, 11 and 14 shall be regarded as preventing the High Contracting Parties from imposing restrictions on the political activity of aliens.

ARTICLE 17

PROHIBITION OF ABUSE OF RIGHTS

Nothing in this Convention may be interpreted as implying for any State, group or person any right to engage in any activity or perform any act aimed at the destruction of any of the rights and freedoms set forth herein or at their limitation to a greater extent than is provided for in the Convention.

ARTICLE 18

LIMITATION ON USE OF RESTRICTIONS ON RIGHTS

The restrictions permitted under this Convention to the said rights and freedoms shall not be applied for any purpose other than those for which they have been prescribed.

Changes to legislation: *There are currently no known outstanding*
effects for the Human Rights Act 1998. (See end of Document for details)

PART II

THE FIRST PROTOCOL

ARTICLE 1

PROTECTION OF PROPERTY

Every natural or legal person is entitled to the peaceful enjoyment of his possessions. No one shall be deprived of his possessions except in the public interest and subject to the conditions provided for by law and by the general principles of international law.

The preceding provisions shall not, however, in any way impair the right of a State to enforce such laws as it deems necessary to control the use of property in accordance with the general interest or to secure the payment of taxes or other contributions or penalties.

ARTICLE 2

RIGHT TO EDUCATION

No person shall be denied the right to education. In the exercise of any functions which it assumes in relation to education and to teaching, the State shall respect the right of parents to ensure such education and teaching in conformity with their own religious and philosophical convictions.

ARTICLE 3

RIGHT TO FREE ELECTIONS

The High Contracting Parties undertake to hold free elections at reasonable intervals by secret ballot, under conditions which will ensure the free expression of the opinion of the people in the choice of the legislature.

[F48 PART 3

ARTICLE 1 OF THE THIRTEENTH PROTOCOL

ABOLITION OF THE DEATH PENALTY

Textual Amendments

F48 Sch. 1 Pt. 3 substituted (22.6.2004) by The Human Rights Act 1998 (Amendment) Order 2004 (S.I. 2004/1574), **art. 2(3)**

The death penalty shall be abolished. No one shall be condemned to such penalty or executed.]

Changes to legislation: There are currently no known outstanding
effects for the Human Rights Act 1998. (See end of Document for details)

PART III

THE SIXTH PROTOCOL

ARTICLE 1

ABOLITION OF THE DEATH PENALTY

ARTICLE 2

DEATH PENALTY IN TIME OF WAR

SCHEDULE 2

Section 10.

REMEDIAL ORDERS

Orders

1   (1) A remedial order may—

    (a)   contain such incidental, supplemental, consequential or transitional provision as the person making it considers appropriate;

    (b)   be made so as to have effect from a date earlier than that on which it is made;

    (c)   make provision for the delegation of specific functions;

    (d)   make different provision for different cases.

(2) The power conferred by sub-paragraph (1)(a) includes—

    (a)   power to amend primary legislation (including primary legislation other than that which contains the incompatible provision); and

    (b)   power to amend or revoke subordinate legislation (including subordinate legislation other than that which contains the incompatible provision).

(3) A remedial order may be made so as to have the same extent as the legislation which it affects.

(4) No person is to be guilty of an offence solely as a result of the retrospective effect of a remedial order.

Procedure

2   No remedial order may be made unless—

    (a)   a draft of the order has been approved by a resolution of each House of Parliament made after the end of the period of 60 days beginning with the day on which the draft was laid; or

    (b)   it is declared in the order that it appears to the person making it that, because of the urgency of the matter, it is necessary to make the order without a draft being so approved.

Changes to legislation: There are currently no known outstanding
effects for the Human Rights Act 1998. (See end of Document for details)

Orders laid in draft

3   (1) No draft may be laid under paragraph 2(a) unless—

  (a)   the person proposing to make the order has laid before Parliament a document which contains a draft of the proposed order and the required information; and

  (b)   the period of 60 days, beginning with the day on which the document required by this sub-paragraph was laid, has ended.

(2) If representations have been made during that period, the draft laid under paragraph 2(a) must be accompanied by a statement containing—

  (a)   a summary of the representations; and

  (b)   if, as a result of the representations, the proposed order has been changed, details of the changes.

Urgent cases

4   (1) If a remedial order ("the original order") is made without being approved in draft, the person making it must lay it before Parliament, accompanied by the required information, after it is made.

(2) If representations have been made during the period of 60 days beginning with the day on which the original order was made, the person making it must (after the end of that period) lay before Parliament a statement containing—

  (a)   a summary of the representations; and

  (b)   if, as a result of the representations, he considers it appropriate to make changes to the original order, details of the changes.

(3) If sub-paragraph (2)(b) applies, the person making the statement must—

  (a)   make a further remedial order replacing the original order; and

  (b)   lay the replacement order before Parliament.

(4) If, at the end of the period of 120 days beginning with the day on which the original order was made, a resolution has not been passed by each House approving the original or replacement order, the order ceases to have effect (but without that affecting anything previously done under either order or the power to make a fresh remedial order).

Definitions

5   In this Schedule—

  "representations" means representations about a remedial order (or proposed remedial order) made to the person making (or proposing to make) it and includes any relevant Parliamentary report or resolution; and

  "required information" means—

  (a)   an explanation of the incompatibility which the order (or proposed order) seeks to remove, including particulars of the relevant declaration, finding or order; and

  (b)   a statement of the reasons for proceeding under section 10 and for making an order in those terms.

Calculating periods

6 In calculating any period for the purposes of this Schedule, no account is to be taken of any time during which—

 (a) Parliament is dissolved or prorogued; or

 (b) both Houses are adjourned for more than four days.

[^{F52}7 (1) This paragraph applies in relation to–

  (a) any remedial order made, and any draft of such an order proposed to be made,–

   (i) by the Scottish Ministers; or

   (ii) within devolved competence (within the meaning of the Scotland Act 1998) by Her Majesty in Council; and

  (b) any document or statement to be laid in connection with such an order (or proposed order).

 (2) This Schedule has effect in relation to any such order (or proposed order), document or statement subject to the following modifications.

 (3) Any reference to Parliament, each House of Parliament or both Houses of Parliament shall be construed as a reference to the Scottish Parliament.

 (4) Paragraph 6 does not apply and instead, in calculating any period for the purposes of this Schedule, no account is to be taken of any time during which the Scottish Parliament is dissolved or is in recess for more than four days.]

Textual Amendments

 F52 Sch. 2 para. 7 inserted (27.7.2000) by S.I. 2000/2040, art. 2, **Sch. Pt. 1 para. 21** (with art. 3)

SCHEDULE 3

Sections 14 and 15.

DEROGATION AND RESERVATION

^{F53F53} PART I

DEROGATION

Textual Amendments

 F53 Sch. 3 Pt. 1 repealed (8.4.2005) by The Human Rights Act 1998 (Amendment) Order 2005 (S.I. 2005/1071), art. 2

United Kingdom's derogation from Article 5(1)

. . . .
. . . .
. . . .–. . . . . .
. . . .

Changes to legislation: *There are currently no known outstanding*
effects for the Human Rights Act 1998. (See end of Document for details)

. . . .

PART II

RESERVATION

At the time of signing the present (First) Protocol, I declare that, in view of certain provisions of the Education Acts in the United Kingdom, the principle affirmed in the second sentence of Article 2 is accepted by the United Kingdom only so far as it is compatible with the provision of efficient instruction and training, and the avoidance of unreasonable public expenditure.

Dated 20 March 1952

Made by the United Kingdom Permanent Representative to the Council of Europe.

SCHEDULE 4

Section 18(6).

JUDICIAL PENSIONS

Duty to make orders about pensions

1   (1) The appropriate Minister must by order make provision with respect to pensions payable to or in respect of any holder of a judicial office who serves as an ECHR judge.

     (2) A pensions order must include such provision as the Minister making it considers is necessary to secure that—

       (a) an ECHR judge who was, immediately before his appointment as an ECHR judge, a member of a judicial pension scheme is entitled to remain as a member of that scheme;

       (b) the terms on which he remains a member of the scheme are those which would have been applicable had he not been appointed as an ECHR judge; and

       (c) entitlement to benefits payable in accordance with the scheme continues to be determined as if, while serving as an ECHR judge, his salary was that which would (but for section 18(4)) have been payable to him in respect of his continuing service as the holder of his judicial office.

Contributions

2   A pensions order may, in particular, make provision—

       (a) for any contributions which are payable by a person who remains a member of a scheme as a result of the order, and which would otherwise be payable by deduction from his salary, to be made otherwise than by deduction from his salary as an ECHR judge; and

       (b) for such contributions to be collected in such manner as may be determined by the administrators of the scheme.

Changes to legislation: There are currently no known outstanding
effects for the Human Rights Act 1998. (See end of Document for details)

Amendments of other enactments

3   A pensions order may amend any provision of, or made under, a pensions Act in such manner and to such extent as the Minister making the order considers necessary or expedient to ensure the proper administration of any scheme to which it relates.

Definitions

4   In this Schedule—

"appropriate Minister" means—

(a) in relation to any judicial office whose jurisdiction is exercisable exclusively in relation to Scotland, the Secretary of State; and

(b) otherwise, the Lord Chancellor;

"ECHR judge" means the holder of a judicial office who is serving as a judge of the Court;

"judicial pension scheme" means a scheme established by and in accordance with a pensions Act;

"pensions Act" means—

(a) the ^{M17}County Courts Act Northern Ireland) 1959;

(b) the ^{M18}Sheriffs' Pensions (Scotland) Act 1961;

(c) the ^{M19}Judicial Pensions Act 1981; or

(d) the ^{M20}Judicial Pensions and Retirement Act 1993;

(e) [^{F54}the Public Service Pensions Act 2013;] and

"pensions order" means an order made under paragraph 1.

Textual Amendments

F54   Words in Sch. 4 para. 4 inserted (1.4.2014) by Public Service Pensions Act 2013 (c. 25), s. 41(2), **Sch. 8 para. 26** (with Sch. 11 para. 8); S.I. 2014/839, art. 4(2)(k)

Marginal Citations

M17   1959 c. 25 (N.I.).

M18   1961 c. 42.

M19   1981 c. 20.

M20   1993 c. 8.

Changes to legislation:
There are currently no known outstanding effects for the Human Rights Act 1998.

Printed in Great Britain
by Amazon

84792875R00031